WALLY & WIND OF THE WOBURN CLIFFS

The True Story of a Peregrine Falcon Family

By John Harrison & Kim Nagy

Also by John Harrison and Kim Nagy

Dead In Good Company:
A Celebration of Mount Auburn Cemetery

True Wildlife Adventure Series for Children

Skylar's Great Adventure
The True Story of a Brave Fresh Pond Owlet

Star Guy's Great Adventure
The True Story of a Salisbury Snowy Owl

Big Caesar's New Home
The True Story of a Coyote Season at Mount Auburn Cemetery

Dedication

Wally is dedicated to the next generation of Peregrine kids.

Mari Hylan, Oscar Kinsman, Sammy Kinsman, Simone Cruz, Henry Elias Maier, Ella Malvey, Benjamin French, Mason George Drudi, Jack Travis Drudi, Oaklyn Elizabeth Drudi, Tennessee Tuttle, Wallis Tuttle, Ella Higginson, Lucille Higginson, Madelyn Roussell, Patrick Roussell, Colin Roussell, Donovan Roussell, Bernadette Roussell, Sophia Matthews, Olivia Matthews, Violet Matthews, Ophelia Matthews, Saoirse Matthews, Canyon Tallman, Carrigan Tallman, Corby Scott Cunningham, Camry Cunningham, Cyler Cunningham, Abigail Parker, Oliver Woolverton Barnett, Olivia Wlodarczyk, Audrey Bradley, Addison Bradley, Amelia Bradley, Nel Rabens, Henry Curth, Nathaniel Nearhood, Caitlin Gower, Nora Gower, Grace Gower, Katherine Rita Sullivan, Cheng-Loong, Cheng-Lin, Saddie Lesso, Adria Hadidian, Eliace Hadidian, Ellieah Marabella, Benjamin Marabella, Joshua Marabella, Francis Santarpio, Haidyn Santarpio, Emme Adams, Everett Burke, Chase Cleary, Elise Drake, Darcy Drennan, Lucas Dunham, Emerson Geranis, Owen Greene, Chris Hedrick, Grey Heredia, Isaiah Iliev-Rovnak, Wyatt Palmer, Isaac Prior, Tyler Ridley, Alyssa Roy, Anna Rutherford, Chloey Succi, Mason Walenta, Ava Walker, Nick Wentworth, Layla Bryan, Ella Bryan, Carter Bryan, Jordan Brennan, John Connors, Thomas Anderson, Sophia Kimber, Ethan Leventhal, Riley Shay Doss, Maddie Lee Dahlbeck, Wyatt Dahlbeck, Grace Hanafin, Charlie Hanafin, Dylan Simard,

Levi Simard, Celine Shedd, Remy Shedd, Elijah Shapiro, Joshua Shapiro, Silvio Ortiz, Brayden Campbell, Jackson Campbell, Bennett Zalinski, Colin Zalinski, August Zalinski, Emma Manning, Jake Manning, Isabella Natalucci, Sophia Natalucci, Gio Natalucci, Declan Haley, Thomas Haley, Shay Shay, Nora Whalen, Brian Whalen, Henry Duval, John Duval, Zayah Asher Perlmutter, Caleb Jack Perlmutter, Mila Sage Perlmutter, Zachary Michael Kaplan, Cameron James Kaplan, Hannah Baron Silva, Ty Minogue, Kaelyn Minogue, Spencer Minogue, Nell Madigan Minogue, Eliana Minogue, Declan Minogue, Hazel Leslie, Lydia Leslie, Justin Williamson, Zinnia Lili Roehl-Gordon, Lamine Gordon, Madeline Rhunette Aandahl, Spencer David Aandahl, Bernadine DeMatteo, Annetta DeMatteo, Maggie Carey, Hugh Carey III, Annie Carey, Sofie Proulx, Sage Proulx, Sky Proulx, Shayne Proulx, Cannon Proulx, Patrick O'Neill, Emma O'Neill, Addison Hale, Isobel Hale, Brooks Camorali, Nathan Robert Gaskill, Pierce Edward Antonsen, Quinlan Grace Hagan, Shea Alice Hagan, Ryann Rose Hagan, Antonio Strate, Jack Sorrentino, Max Sorrentino, Mary Abigail McElwreath, Caroline Marguerite McElwreath, Evelyn Rose Riggs, Corinne Grace Riggs, Norah Lynn Riggs, Hailey Rene Riggs, Rhea Coogan, Della Coogan, Adrian Vogel, Sage Vogel, Oliver Vogel, Bailey Rose Sherman, Vivienne Sophia Sherman, Rose Charlotte Baker, Madeline DiGiorgio, Amelia DiGiorgio, Jocelyn Gesner, Ian Gesner, Evelyn Lamer, Owen Lamer, Ivan Lakits, Camille Horstman, Chesney Schlereth, Violet Nina, Noah Allen, Jude Allen and the grandchildren of the Boston Admirals Club employees.

On a cold and windy December morning, a pair of Peregrine Falcons perched on the granite cliffs in the town of Woburn, Massachusetts. They were immune to the cold and wind, because they were insulated by their feathers and the soft down underneath. They could fluff up their feathers, which created air pockets that kept them warm.

The male Peregrine had come to be called Wally by those who watched him. He had lived on these cliffs for several years. Peregrine Falcons prefer living on cliffs, because there are fissures, outcroppings and ledges where they can hide and nest.

If you observed Wally and Wind, his mate, through binoculars, you would notice that they constantly monitored their environment: they looked left and right; up and down; back and forth. Peregrine Falcons need to know what is going on around them at all times, for there are many dangers. This constant vigilance is what keeps them safe.

What is a threat for Peregrine Falcons? Other predatory birds. Sometimes a hawk or an eagle will fly close to their cliff home. When this happens, Wally and Wind would pursue the intruder and chase it away. They don't allow other big birds into their territory. They protect their home!

Since they will raise their family on these cliffs, their neighborhood must be free of dangers. Chasing away potentially threatening birds - even other Peregrines - gets the message out to STAY AWAY. Once their chicks hatch, they become more aggressive in protecting their habitat.

What else could you notice if you watched them? They preen, or groom, often. They take excellent care of their feathers, which protect, and even waterproof them. They use their beaks to position feathers, or lock feathers that have become separated. They also clean their plumage, a bird's feather covering, to keep the feathers neat and organized. Preening keeps them in top condition for flight.

If the falcons landed on nearby light and telephone poles, you could watch them preen up close. They might stay on these poles for more than an hour! It was a great way for watchers to observe their behavior.

The Peregrines had everything they needed to thrive - food, water and shelter.

What do Peregrine Falcons eat? Mostly they eat smaller birds that they overtake (or catch) in flight. With their superior vision, Peregrines can see prey far away.

What is unique about Peregrine Falcons? They are the fastest animal on earth. When they spot prey from high above in the sky, they go into a dive, called a stoop. They tuck in their wings, accelerate, and can reach speeds of over 200 miles an hour. Watching them fly around their Woburn cliffs home was exciting!

Eventually the long and cold winter ended, and then it was spring. The Peregrines were planning for a family, so they made a scrape in the loose sand and gravel to hold their eggs. It had to be safe and protected from the elements.

27

Why is a Peregrine falcon's nest called a scrape? It's because the parents scrape out a depression, or bowl, at the nest site. This keeps the eggs from rolling off the cliff. It also provides a border to hold heat during the approximately month-long incubation period. The scrape is about nine inches in diameter and about two inches deep. This is a very different nest from hawks, eagles and owls!

29

Soon Wind was sitting on her eggs. Wally brought food to her. He also sat on the eggs at times so Wind could get exercise.

One day, the first chick hatched! Over the next several days, more chicks hatched, until there were four. Wally would have to work hard to feed his big family!

The chicks were born covered with soft, cotton-like down. They looked comical with their over-sized heads and awkward bodies, but not for long! As they grew, Wind was able to leave the nest, and both parents hunted. The chicks ate a lot and they were always hungry.

Birds are often banded on their legs, which is like putting a ring on our fingers. These numbered and lettered bands help to track them so wildlife experts can monitor their travel patterns. Banding helps us learn more about birds.

But how would these Peregrine chicks get banded, living so high on the cliffs?

On the morning of June 18, Tom French of MassWildlife, and his assistants, Jesse Caney and Travis Drudi, arrived at the cliffs. Jesse Caney rappelled down to the nest. Wally and Wind flew around, agitated. They almost brushed Jesse's head. That is why he wore a helmet and protective sunglasses.

Jesse carefully gathered all four chicks, and put them in a canvas bag. He lowered the bag to Travis Drudi, who waited below.

On the ground, many people and photographers watched. It was so exciting!

45

Each chick got one band from the federal agency, and one band from the state. It was important to put the right bands on males and females. Female raptors are generally 30% larger than males. You wouldn't want to put a male band on a female leg! They discovered that there were three males and one female. The female was the smallest because she was born last, but still she needed a larger band.

Tom French and his assistants worked quickly. Soon the chicks were placed back in the canvas bag and Jesse climbed the rope back up to the nest and carefully placed each chick on the nest. Within a few minutes, Wind landed next to her chicks, and everything quieted down.

Soon the chicks, one by one, fledged. Fledging is their first flight; the most important day in a young bird's life! All of the photographers below waited patiently for hours, hoping to catch this special moment!

Once they fledged, the chicks learned very quickly. The parents flew with them, teaching them the ways of the air and the mechanics of flight. The parents even exchanged food with the young fledglings, high up in the sky!

The little female, the last chick to hatch, lagged behind her brothers. She was having trouble keeping up, since she was the youngest. Her brothers took off together, racing through the sky, and they left her far behind. Sometimes she clung to the cliffs. Wind would encourage her to fly, but she was uncertain.

Then one day she became confident - and she fledged! Soon she could fly as fast as her brothers, and the whole family flew together, high up in the sky above the Woburn cliffs.

Day after day, for most of the summer, the photographers enjoyed this wonderful air show. They watched the Peregrine family fly, and sometimes, on hot days, the Peregrines cooled off in puddles of water!

The chicks would stay with their parents to learn valuable hunting skills, and then in the fall, they would disburse to find their own territories, and their own mates. Then they would be ready to start their own families, and continue the Peregrine circle of life.

Tufts Wildlife Clinic

Wild animals get sick and injured just like us. Is there a hospital for them? Yes, there is. One of the best hospitals for wild animals is Tufts Wildlife Clinic at Cummings Veterinary Medical Center at Tufts University in Grafton, Massachusetts, about 40 miles from Wally and Wind's neighborhood in Woburn.

Tufts Wildlife Clinic at Cummings Veterinary Medical Center at Tufts University (credit: Alonso Nichols/Tufts University)

Tufts Wildlife Clinic is located at Cummings School of Veterinary Medicine, a school that trains veterinarians — doctors who care for and treat animals. The Wildlife Clinic helps sick and injured native New England wildlife. Most of the animal patients are birds — from very small birds to large raptors; hawks, eagles, falcons and owls. Small birds often become injured falling out of the nest before they fledge (fledging is a bird's first flight from its nest). Other times they can be injured when they fledge. Pets — especially cats — can be another source of injury for small birds. Really, cats should stay indoors — it's better for the birds and better for the cats too.

A flight barn at Tufts Wildlife Clinic at Cummings Veterinary Medical Center at Tufts University (credit: Alonso Nichols/Tufts University)

The big raptors (also called birds of prey) that are brought to Tufts Wildlife Clinic usually have injured wings or head injuries. This is often from crashing into cars, which breaks bones and causes concussions. According to the veterinarians at the clinic, birds are the best healers. Why? Broken bones take about three weeks to heal for birds, and six to eight weeks for mammals.

A flight barn at Tufts Wildlife Clinic at Cummings Veterinary Medical Center at Tufts University (credit: Alonso Nichols/Tufts University)

The veterinarians at Tufts Wildlife Clinic help fix the broken wings and perform surgery when necessary. When the birds grow stronger, they have physical therapy in smaller flight pens then in the larger 'flight barn.' The flight barn is 100 feet long, 40 feet high and 40 feet wide. The birds fly, little by little, in this flight barn, until they are strong enough to be released back into the wild. This can take anywhere from two to three weeks. It is always the goal of the hospital veterinarians and staff to release animals back into to the wild where they belong.

A Great Horned Owl perches in a flight pen at Tufts Wildlife Clinic at Cummings Veterinary Medical Center at Tufts University (credit: Alonso Nichols/Tufts University)

If a person brings an injured raptor to the clinic, the staff will often allow that person to release the bird back into the wild if the bird is completely healed. Ideally the bird is released near where it was found, since this is probably its 'home base' neighborhood. In 2011, Cambridge resident and birder Susan Moses brought in an injured Red-tailed Hawk that she found in Cambridge. This hawk was one of a pair of Red-tails that had nested on a ledge on Oxford Street in Cambridge at the Harvard School of Engineering and Applied Sciences.

A juvenile Peregrine Falcon perches in a flight pen at Tufts Wildlife
Clinic at Cummings Veterinary Medical Center at Tufts University
(credit: Alonso Nichols/Tufts University).

The clinic's veterinarians and staff treated the hawk's injuries. When it was fully recovered, Susan released that hawk on the lawn of the Harvard Museum of Natural History, across the street from the School of Engineering and Applied Sciences ledge nest. It was exciting to witness the release. The hawk was let out of the box facing in the direction of the nest. It immediately flew up to its mate, then they flew together again.

A Red-tailed Hawk rehabilitates in a flight pen at Tufts Wildlife Clinic at Cummings Veterinary Medical Center at Tufts University (credit: Anna Miller/Tufts University)

The Tufts Wildlife Clinic restored this hawk's health. They help other animals in this way, every day. At any one time there might be as many as one hundred animals being treated at the facility; over the course of a year, about four thousand are seen at the clinic. This special organization works miracles with the animals that are brought to them. We and the animals are so fortunate to have this wonderful clinic nearby.

A Bald Eagle rehabilitates in a flight barn at Tufts Wildlife Clinic at Cummings Veterinary Medical Center at Tufts University (credit: Alonso Nichols/Tufts University)

A Red-tailed Hawk is held for examination at Tufts Wildlife Clinic
at Cummings Veterinary Medical Center at Tufts University
(credit: Melody Ko/Tufts University)

Susan Moses, on the lawn of the Harvard Museum of Natural History, releases the Red-tailed Hawk that she brought to Tufts Wildlife Clinic to be treated for injuries.

Woburn's Cummings Foundation

When Wally and Wind fly above the Woburn cliffs, they can see the headquarters of Woburn's Cummings Foundation Inc. at 200 West Cummings Park. This foundation has accomplished many wonderful things, including the establishment of The Cummings School of Veterinary Medicine At Tufts in Grafton, MA; the premiere institution of its kind in the country. The Cummings School of Veterinary Medicine is able to help Wally and Wind and any other animal in New England that is sick or injured and needs expert medical care.

The foundation was established in 1986, and is an outgrowth of Cummings Properties, founded by Bill Cummings in 1970. Since its founding, the organization has awarded more than $250 million dollars in grants to Greater Boston nonprofits alone - for human services, education, healthcare and social justice. The foundation's reach extends as far as East Africa, aiding in Rwanda's post-genocide recovery and rebuilding.

In May of 2011, Bill & Joyce Cummings joined The Giving Pledge, an organization founded by Bill and Melinda Gates and Warren Buffet. Some of the world's wealthiest individuals have pledged to donate at least half of their assets for philanthropic purposes through this organization. Learn more about Bill Cummings in his book <u>Starting Small and Making It Big: An Entrepreneur's Journey to Billion-Dollar Philanthropist</u>.

Perhaps when Wally and Wind fly over the Woburn cliffs, they give a nod to honor the Cummings Foundation. We should all honor this Foundation, which has contributed so much to our communities.

PEREGRINE FALCON FACTS

- The word "peregrine" means one who wanders. The scientific name for the Peregrine Falcon is Falco peregrinus anatum.

- The Peregrine Falcon nearly became extinct because of the use of DDT and other pesticides. The eggshells became weak, and they would break. Banning DDT has helped the Peregrine population rebound, as well as other raptors.

- The average life span in the wild is up to 17 years.

- Peregrines are favored by falconers, and have been used in that sport for many centuries.

- Peregrines measure 14-19 inches with a wingspan of 3.3 to 3.6 feet.

- Female Peregrines are larger than males. The male Peregrine is called a "tercel," because he is one-third smaller than the female.

- Many Peregrines migrate. Those that nest on Arctic tundra and winter in South America fly as many as 15,500 miles in a year!

- Peregrines have a strong homing instinct that leads them back to favored aeries.

- You can help Peregrines, other birds, yourselves and the environment by eating fruits and vegetables that have not been sprayed with pesticides and herbicides.

ACKNOWLEDGMENTS

We give special thanks to our first readers: Bobbie Gatz, Dr. Mariana Castells, Sharon Sherman, Corinne Kinsman, Mari Hylan, Dr. Maynard Suffredini, Jr., Don and Geri Tremblay and Tom French, Ph D.

Our gratitude for: Corinne and Artty Kinsman, Peter Filichia, Linda Konner, Paul Treseler, Ray and Deb Cilley, Bob and Edie Di Giorgio, James Harrison, Mary Hogan, Joe Plati, Joe and Karen Polvere, Keith and Cathy Joyce, Bob and Becky Parsons, Mark Nickerson, Craig Gibson, Ray Brown of Talkin' Birds, Upton Bell, JoAnne O'Neill, Gary Goshgarian, William Martin, Cathy and Dick Minogue, Jeanne Bohen, Susan Hershey, Sandy Selesky, Lloyd and Joyce Torgove, Frank and Bobbie Gatz, John Amaral, Sangeet Kaur Khalsa, Hank Phillippi Ryan, Jim and Patty Sears-Joyce, Sharon Kennedy, Dawna Blum of Wild Birds Unlimited, our Wildlife Whisperer John Sullivan and - Steve Gladstone, who brings ideas and manuscripts to life.

Special thanks to our True Wildlife Adventures team member Mari Hylan for naming Wind.

Special thanks to Craig Gibson, our Peregrine Whisperer, who founded the Peregrine Monitor Group, which has been chronicling the life cycle of the Woburn Peregrines since 2018. And thanks to the group members who participated in this project. Wally and Wind and their generations of kids have become family to all of us.

We thank Hunt's Photo and Video of Melrose for sponsoring the Peregrine Monitor Group exhibit and reception in November of 2018 and for being the go-to store for our photography needs.

We thank Tufts Wildlife Clinic's Taraneh Pettinato, Associate Director of Media Relations, and Dr. Maureen Murray, for their time and efforts in our celebration of their essential institution. Thank you Michael Armanious, Jeff Barnd, Jeff Munro, Jonathan Barbato and Katie Chang of Arlington Community Media.

And lastly, in loving memory of our friends in wildlife Ernie Sarro and Virginia Parsons.

PHOTO CREDITS

- John Harrison: back cover and pages 3, 13, 19, 27, 31, 33, 41, 43, 45, 47, 49, 57, and 65.
- Kim Nagy: front cover and pages 7, 17, 55, and 64.
- Joe Callanan: page 9
- Maryjane Keeler: page 11
- Harold Roussell: page 15
- John Blout: page 21
- Changde Wu: page 23
- Jim Renault: page 25
- Stan Deutsch: page 29
- Andy Kawa: page 35
- Nancy Gower: page 37
- Jay Richard: page 39
- Craig Gibson: page 51
- Ken Proulx: page 53
- David Morris: page 59
- Gregg Ohanian: page 61
- Chris He: 62
- Judd Nathan: page 63
- Leigh Scott: page 66
- Photo conversion to illustration by Steve Gladstone

ABOUT THE AUTHORS

John Harrison and Kim Nagy are the Editors of *Dead in Good Company,* a compelling collection of essays, poems and wildlife photographs of Mount Auburn Cemetery in Cambridge, Massachusetts. Sweet Auburn, as it's affectionately known, is America's first garden cemetery, and *Dead in Good Company* is the first book to celebrate the Cemetery as a place of regeneration and transformation; the circle of life. Mount Auburn Cemetery is one of New England's Birding Hotspots.

Skylar's Great Adventure: The True Story of a Brave Fresh Pond Owlet, Star Guy's Great Adventure: The True Story of a Salisbury Snowy Owl, and *Big Caesar's New Home: The True Story of a Coyote Season at Mount Auburn Cemetery* are the first three books in the True Wildlife Adventure series.

See more at: www.facebook.com/deadingoodcompany and on YouTube:

https://www.youtube.com/watch?v=cFwi69Uk2-4&feature=youtu.be&app=desktop

John Harrison Founded Epilog Enterprises, a book distribution company, in 1975. His passion for nature ultimately led to the idea for this book. His photographs have been published by Mass Audubon, the Humane Society of the United States, and Project Coyote in CA, and have appeared in books, calendars, magazines, newspapers, and websites. He lectures on nature and wildlife at elementary schools and to senior citizen groups. Additionally, he authored the *Medford Wildlife Watch* blog for The Medford Transcript newspaper for ten years (Photo by Rick Olick).

Kim Nagy has made the natural world both her profession and her hobby. She is an avid wildlife and nature photographer, and travels widely in pursuit of her craft. She works as a National Sales Manager in the natural products industry. Her photos have appeared in National Geographic's Daily Dozen, *BirdWatching, The BirdNote* calendar, several publications of the Massachusetts Audubon Society, *The Marco Review, Tin Mountain Conservation Center* and more.

See more at: www.facebook.com/catchlightphotos

Made in the USA
Middletown, DE
25 July 2020